FEATURED PROJECTS

These brief project instructions may help you pick out the type of project you'd like to create using your favorite transfer. See Techniques (pgs. 8 and 9) for more detailed information.

Front Cover

Gardening Apron and Gloves (transfers on pg. 21)
- Paint designs on a purchased apron and gloves using *fabric paints*.
- *Sponge paint* apron and gloves around designs using fabric paint.
- Attach jewel stones to designs using puddles of dimensional fabric paint for some and jewel glue for others.
- Add accents using *dimensional fabric paints*.
- Add *glitter* to petals.
- Sew lace along top edge of apron and cuffs of gloves.
- Pin silk flowers to apron.

Teatime Pillow (transfer on pg. 63)
- Paint design on a Battenberg doily using *fabric paints*.
- Add details using *dimensional fabric paints*.
- Hand sew doily to pillow front.
- Hot glue silk flowers and ribbon bows to pillow front.

Birdhouse Wreath (transfers on pg. 37)
- Make *canvas cutouts* using *acrylic paints* and *dimensional fabric paints*.
- Hot glue canvas cutouts, artificial flowers and leaves, and ribbon bows to wreath.

Birdhouse Plant Pokes (transfers on pg. 40)
- Make *canvas cutout* using *acrylic paints* and *dimensional fabric paints*.
- Glue cutout to a stick.
- Tie a bow around stick below cutout.

Unicorn Handbag (transfer on pg. 106)
- Paint design on a purchased canvas handbag using *fabric paints*.
- Add accents using *dimensional fabric paint*.
- Add *glitter* to design.
- Attach jewel stones to handbag using puddles of dimensional paint.
- Tie various width ribbons into a bow around handle.

Carousel Horses Boxer Shorts (transfers on pgs. 107 and 108)
- Paint design on boxer shorts using *fabric paints*.
- Add accents using *dimensional fabric paints*.
- Sew lace around leg openings of boxer shorts.

Back Cover

Independence Day Shirt (transfer on pg. 124)
- Paint design on a T-shirt using *fabric paints*.
- Add pizzazz using *dimensional fabric paints*.
- Attach jewel stones to shirt using jewel glue.
- Add *glitter* to design.
- Glue three rows of metallic ribbon along each shoulder seam to resemble epaulets.
- Glue a jewel stone at each end of metallic ribbon lengths.
- Knot various lengths and widths of ribbons and torn fabric strips in center; pin to shoulders.

Christmas Shoes (transfers on pg. 159)
- Paint designs on canvas shoes using *fabric paints*.
- Add accents using *dimensional fabric paints*, adding glitter while paint is still wet. Shake off excess glitter when dry.
- Attach jewel stones to shoes using puddles of dimensional paint.
- Lace shoes with metallic ribbon.

Poinsettia Boxes (transfer on pg. 152)
- Spray a papier-mâché box with spray primer.
- Paint box a solid color using *acrylic paint*.
- *Sponge paint* box using gold metallic acrylic paint.
- Paint design on box lid using *acrylic paints*.
- Outline design using *dimensional fabric paint*, adding glitter while paint is still wet. Shake off excess glitter when dry.
- Attach jewel stones to box using puddles of dimensional paint.
- Hot glue trim around sides of box lid.

Classy Teacher Sweatshirt (transfers on pg. 126)
- Paint design on a sweatshirt using *fabric paints*.
- Add details using *dimensional fabric paints*.
- Sew ribbon bows to sweatshirt.

Boot-scootin' Vest (transfers on pg. 57)
- Paint designs on a denim vest using *fabric paints*.
- Add accents using *dimensional fabric paints*.
- Add decorative nailheads.

Page 2

Conversation Hearts Shirt (transfers on pg. 117)
- Paint designs on a T-shirt using *fabric paints*.
- Add *glitter* to hearts.
- Add embellishments to designs using *dimensional fabric paints*.
- Cut off hem of shirt. Fringe bottom edge of shirt.
- Add a bead to some fringe lengths, using knots to hold beads in place.

Happy Easter Sweatshirt (transfer on pg. 120)
- Paint design on sweatshirt using *fabric paints*.
- Add words and embellishments using *dimensional fabric paints* and adding glitter to embellishments while paint is still wet. Shake off excess glitter when dry.

Snowman Sweatshirt (transfer on pg. 140)
- Paint design on a sweatshirt using *fabric paints*.
- Accent design using *dimensional fabric paints*.
- Add *glitter* to design.
- Attach jewel stones to sweatshirt using jewel glue or puddles of dimensional fabric paint.
- Pin a metallic ribbon bow to shoulder.

Birdhouses Peg Rack (transfer on pg. 36)
- Paint design on a piece of fabric using *acrylic paints*.
- Add accents using *dimensional fabric paints*.
- Make a *padded shape* and insert into peg rack opening.
- Glue a length of rickrack across front of peg rack.

Barnyard Border Baskets (transfers on pg. 53)
- Paint design on a strip of white fabric using *acrylic paints*.
- Press edges of fabric strip to wrong side.
- Glue rickrack along long edges.
- Glue fabric strip around basket.

Home Sweet Home Picture (transfer on pg. 50)
- Paint a purchased canvas panel a solid color using *acrylic paint*.
- Paint design using acrylic paints.
- Fuse fabric strips to frame using paper-backed fusible web.
- Glue rickrack and lace to edges of frame.
- Glue painted wooden hearts to corners of frame.
- Insert canvas panel in frame.

Country Dish Towels (transfers on pg. 51 and 76)
- Paint design on a purchased dish towel using *fabric paints*.
- Sew a length of lace across lower edge of towel; sew metallic rickrack across top of lace.

Pot of Tulips Shirt (transfer on pg. 16)
- Paint design on a T-shirt using *fabric paints*.
- Scatter dots of *dimensional fabric paints*.
- Attach jewel stones to shirt using puddles of dimensional paint.
- Sew lace around sleeves of shirt; pin lace bows to shirt.

Page 3

Snowman Ornaments (transfers on pg. 155)
- Paint design on wooden heart using *acrylic paints*.
- Seal ornament using matte-finish clear acrylic spray sealer.
- Add details to design using *dimensional fabric paint*, adding glitter while paint is still wet. Shake off excess glitter when dry.
- Add a twisted satin cord for a hanger.

Halloween Ghost Sweatshirt (transfer on pg. 133)
- Paint design on a sweatshirt using *fabric paints*.
- Add *glitter* to ghost and stars.
- Attach jewel stones to sweatshirt using puddles of dimensional fabric paint.
- Add details using *dimensional fabric paint*.

God Bless America Banner (transfer on pg. 123)
- Paint design on a purchased banner using *fabric paints*.
- Add words and details using *dimensional fabric paints*.
- Attach a metallic wire star garland hanger.

Noah's Ark Shirt (transfer on pg. 84)
- Paint design on a T-shirt using *fabric paints*.
- Sew buttons to shirt.
- Add *glitter* to shirt and buttons.
- Add words using *dimensional fabric paint*.
- Sew lace around sleeves; pin lace bows to shirt.

Christmas Dress (transfers on pg. 159)
- Paint design on a sweatshirt dress using *fabric paints*.
- Attach jewel stones to dress using puddles of dimensional paint.
- Add embellishments using *dimensional fabric paints*, adding glitter while paint is still wet. Shake off excess glitter when dry.
- Sew jumbo metallic rickrack along hemline.
- Tie two ribbons together into a bow; pin to waistline of dress.

Page 4

Love My Dog Chalkboard (transfer on pg. 82)
- Paint design on a piece of fabric using *acrylic paints*.
- Make a *padded shape* and insert into chalkboard opening.
- Seal dog biscuits with matte-finish clear acrylic spray sealer; hot glue to chalkboard.

Noah's Ark Pillow (transfer on pg. 85)
- Paint design on a purchased pillow sham using *fabric paints*.
- Add accents using *dimensional fabric paints*.
- Add *glitter* to design.
- Cut fabric strips using pinking shears; fuse to pillow sham using paper-backed fusible web tape.
- Hot glue buttons to corners.

Indian Corn Pillow (transfer on pg. 138)
- Paint design on a piece of fabric using *fabric paints*.
- Add corn kernels using *dimensional fabric paints*.
- Fringe raw edges of fabric.
- Stitch fabric to pillow front using embroidery floss.

Boy's Best Friend Sweat Suit (transfers on pgs. 80 and 81)
- Paint designs on a sweatshirt and sweat pants using *fabric paints*.

Seed Packet Place Mats (transfers on pg. 23)
- *Sponge paint* purchased polyester canvas place mat using *fabric paints*.
- Paint design on place mat using fabric paints.
- Sew gathered lace to edge of place mat.

Rather Be Fishing Shirt (transfer on pg. 110)
- Paint design on a T-shirt using *fabric paints*.

Page 5

Ice Cream Cones Shirt (transfers on pg. 100)
- Paint designs on a T-shirt using *fabric paints*.
- Add words and details using *dimensional fabric paints*.

Beach Bag (transfers on pg. 88)
- Paint design on a purchased tote bag using *fabric paints*.
- Add words and detail lines using *dimensional fabric paints*.
- Tie various ribbon lengths into a bow; hot glue to handle.
- Attach pearls to tote bag and bow using puddles of dimensional paint.
- Add *glitter* to tote bag and bow.

Teddy Bear Hangers (transfers on pg. 95)
- Paint a purchased wooden hanger a solid color using *acrylic paints*.
- Paint design using *acrylic paints*.
- *Sponge paint* hanger around design using acrylic paints.
- Tie a ribbon bow at top of hanger.

Little Angel Bibs (transfers on pg. 67)
- Paint design on a purchased bib using *fabric paints*.
- Sew rickrack around edges of bib.

Milking Stool (transfer on pg. 97)
- Paint a wooden stool a solid color using *acrylic paints*. Paint stool seat another color.
- Paint design using acrylic paints.
- Cut a sponge into a cow spot shape and *sponge paint* cow spots on legs of stool using acrylic paint.
- Add *glitter* to stool seat.
- Apply two coats of acrylic spray sealer to stool.

Teddy Bear Tote Bag (transfer on pg. 90)
- Paint design on a purchased tote bag using *fabric paints*.
- Sew rows of gathered lace around top of tote bag.
- Glue rickrack around edges of design using fabric glue.
- Glue buttons to corners of design using jewel glue.

TECHNIQUES
TRANSFERRING DESIGNS
Transferring to Fabric or Primed Canvas

Before transferring your design, use one of the small test transfers included throughout the book to help you determine the best iron temperature and length of time needed to achieve a good transfer.

1. If you are transferring a design to a fabric item that will be washed, first wash and dry the item without using fabric softener.
2. Preheat iron for five minutes on appropriate setting for fabric or canvas being used. Do **not** use steam.
3. Since transfer ink may bleed through fabric, place a clean piece of fabric or paper under the design area.
4. Place transfer, **inked side down**, on **right side** of fabric or canvas. Place iron on transfer; hold for five seconds. Do **not** slide iron. Pick up iron and move to another position on transfer so areas under steam holes are transferred. Carefully lift one corner of transfer to see if design has been transferred. If not, place iron on transfer a few more seconds.

5. To transfer the design to a dark-colored fabric, trace the design onto tracing paper. Place tracing paper, traced side down, on **right side** of fabric; pin in place. Insert a light colored transfer paper (such as Saral®), **coated side down**, under tracing paper. Use a stylus or a dull pencil to draw over lines of design.

Transferring to Paper

Before transferring your design, use one of the small test transfers included throughout the book to help you determine the best iron temperature and length of time needed to achieve a good transfer.

1. Preheat iron for five minutes on appropriate setting for paper being used. Do **not** use steam.
2. Place transfer, **inked side down**, on **right side** of paper. Place iron on transfer; hold for five seconds. Do **not** slide iron. Pick up iron and move to another position on transfer so areas under steam holes are transferred.

Transferring to Wood

1. To prepare wood, sand the wood until smooth; remove sanding dust with a tack cloth. Basecoat wood if desired, applying several coats of paint if necessary.
2. Trace the design onto tracing paper.
3. Place tracing paper, **traced side down**, on wood; tape in place. Insert transfer paper (such as graphite paper or Saral®), **coated side down**, under tracing paper. Use a stylus or a dull pencil to draw over lines of design.

PAINTING FABRIC

1. To stabilize fabric, iron freezer paper (coated side toward fabric) to wrong side of fabric under area to be painted. Place a waxed T-shirt form beneath fabric; secure with T-pins.
2. If item will be laundered, paint design with either fabric paint or a mixture of half textile medium and half acrylic paint. If item will not be laundered, paint design with acrylic paint.
3. Outline and add accents with a permanent felt-tip pen or a liner paintbrush and paint.
4. Follow paint manufacturer's instructions to heat-set and launder.

USING DIMENSIONAL FABRIC PAINTS

Dimensional paints are excellent for outlining, adding dots or other small accents, or using anywhere you want to add a raised look to the design.

1. Turn the bottle upside down and let paint fill the tip to keep the paint flowing smoothly.
2. Clean the tip often with a paper towel.

3. If the tip becomes clogged, insert a straight pin into the opening or remove the tip and clean with warm water.
4. If a mistake is made, use a paring knife to gently scrape off paint before it dries; remove stain with non-acetone nail polish remover or soap and water. Or, camouflage the mistake by incorporating it into the design.
5. Keep painted project lying flat at least 24 hours to allow the dimensional paint to sufficiently set before handling.

SPONGE PAINTING

1. Wet sponge; squeeze out excess water. Pour paint on plate. Dip sponge in paint; do not saturate. Dab sponge on paper towel to remove excess paint.
2. Place sponge on surface to be painted. Lightly press sponge on surface; remove sponge. Allow to dry.

PAINTING WOOD

1. Paint design with acrylic paint.
2. Outline and add detail lines with a liner paintbrush and paint. *(**Note:** A permanent felt-tip pen may bleed into the wood grain.)*
3. Seal the wood using a clear polyurethane spray sealer.

ADDING GLITTER

1. Use a paintbrush to apply craft or fabric glue wherever you wish to add glitter.
2. While the glue is still wet, generously sprinkle area with glitter.
3. When dry, shake off excess glitter.

MAKING CANVAS CUTOUTS

We recommend using primed canvas. This will save you the time and mess of priming it yourself. It is pre-shrunk and ready to use.

1. Cut two pieces of primed canvas ½" larger on all sides than design. Cut a piece of paper-backed fusible web slightly smaller than canvas piece. Fuse web to wrong side of one piece of canvas; remove paper backing. Fuse web side of canvas piece to wrong side of remaining canvas piece.
2. Transfer and paint design on canvas.
3. Cut out.

MAKING A PADDED SHAPE

1. Cut a piece of poster board or mat board and a piece of batting the desired finished size. Hot glue batting to board.
2. Center board, batting side down, on wrong side of painted fabric. Fold fabric over edges of board; hot glue in place.

Aleene's®
Test Transfer

10

Aleene's®
Test Transfer

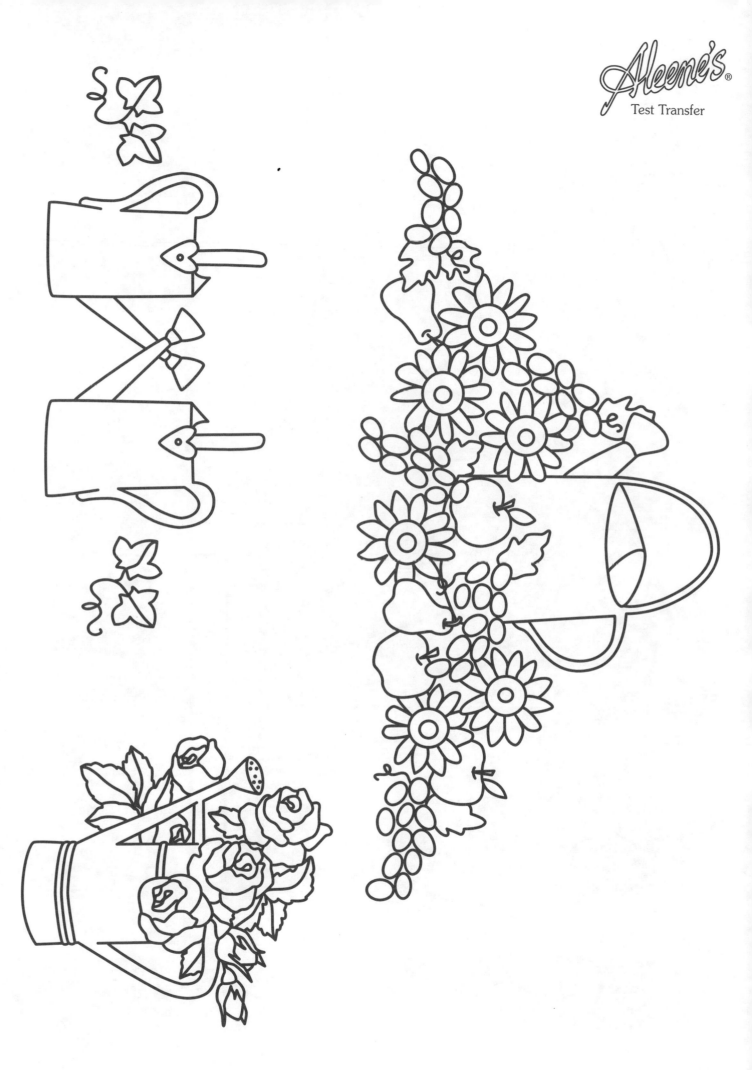

15

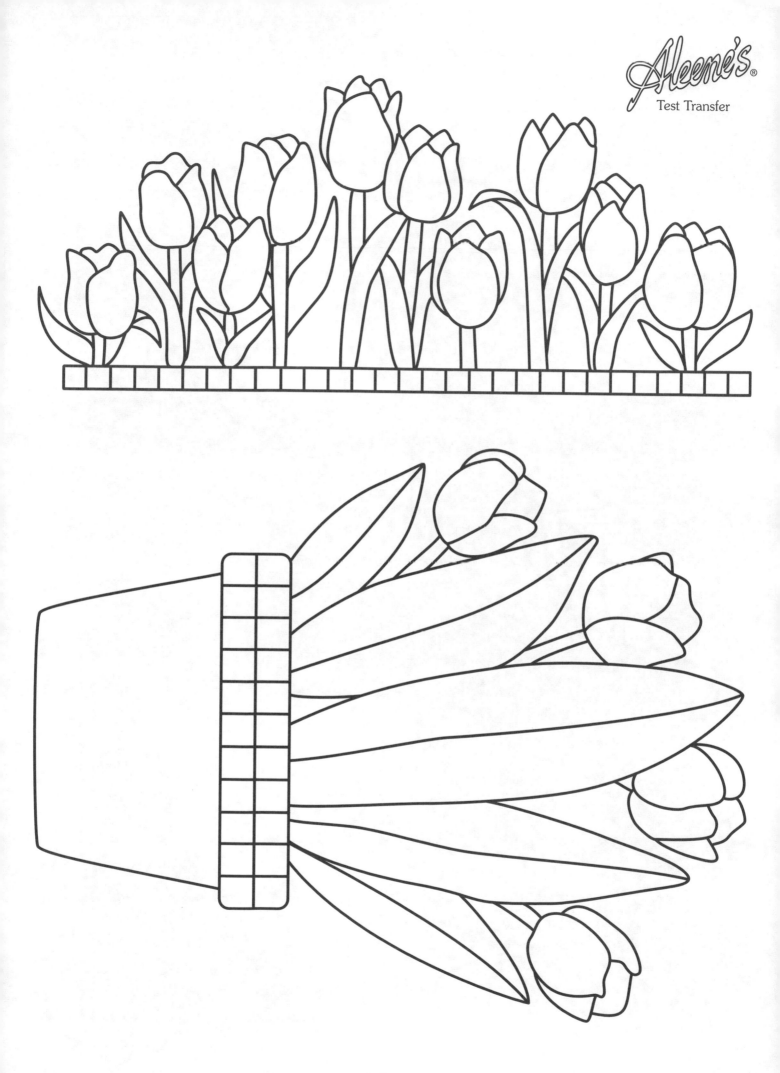

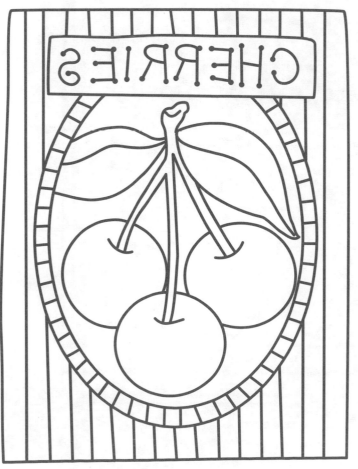

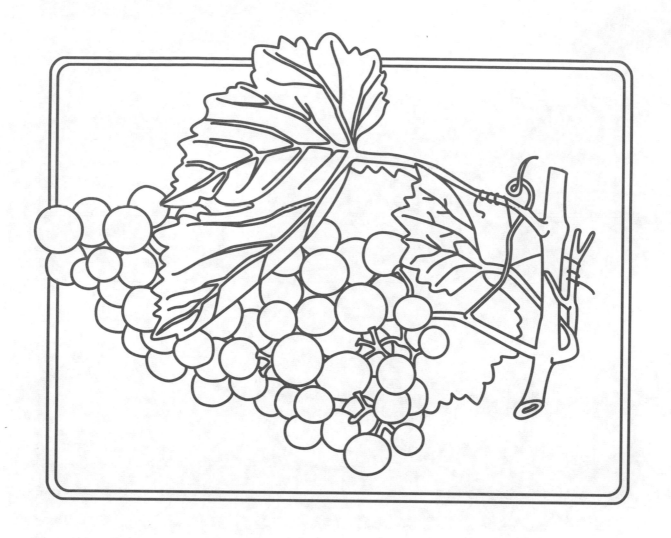

26

GATHER LOVE
PLANT KINDNESS

Happiness is homegrown

WELCOME

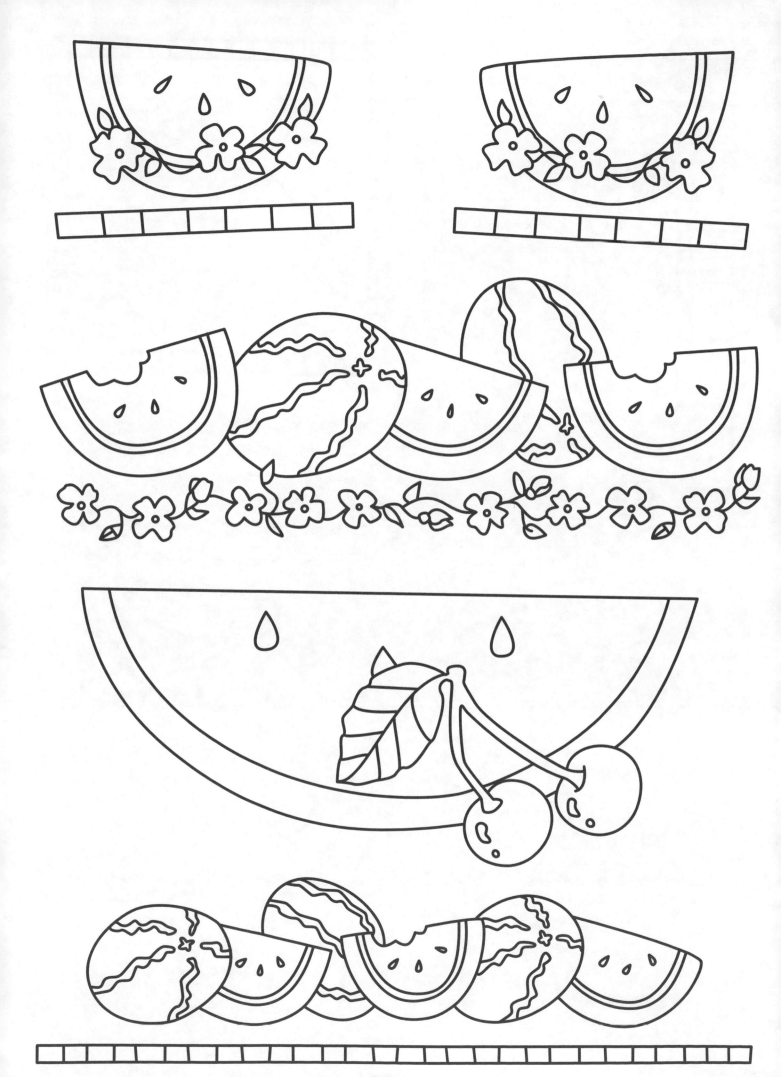

34

35

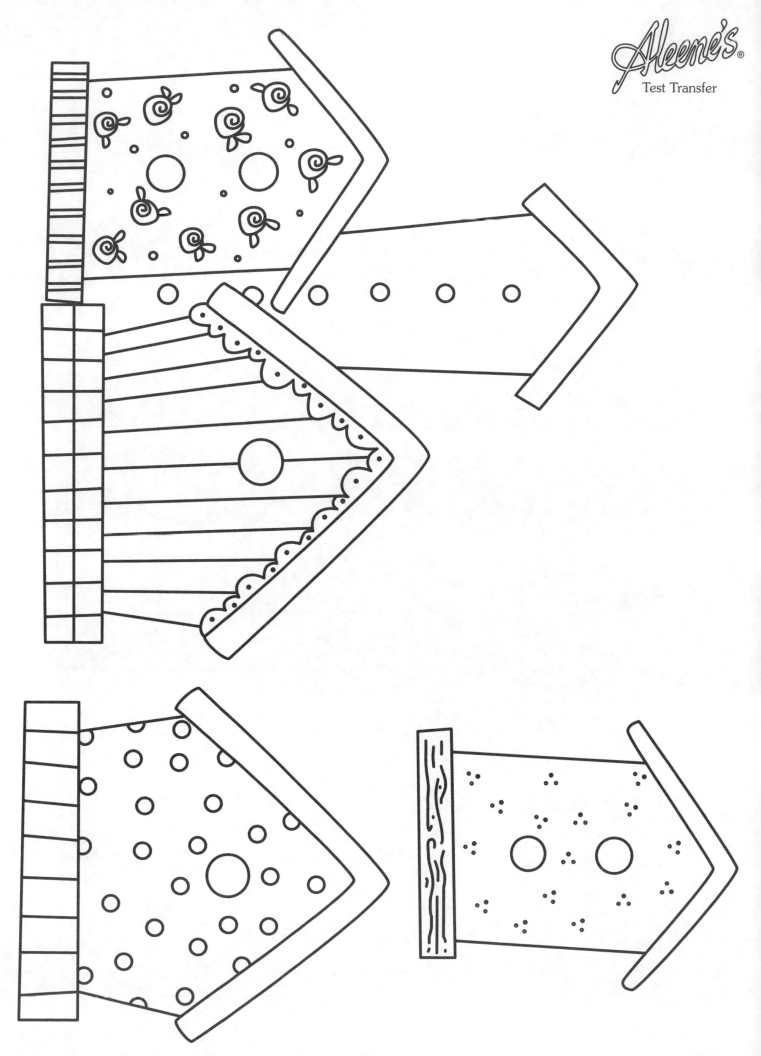

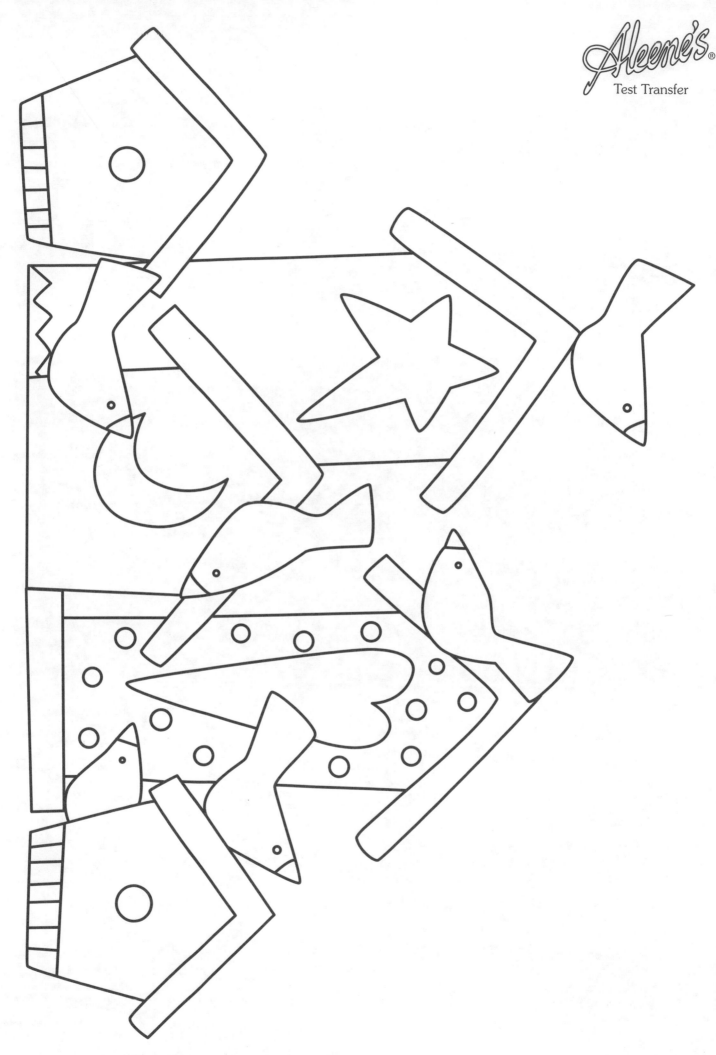

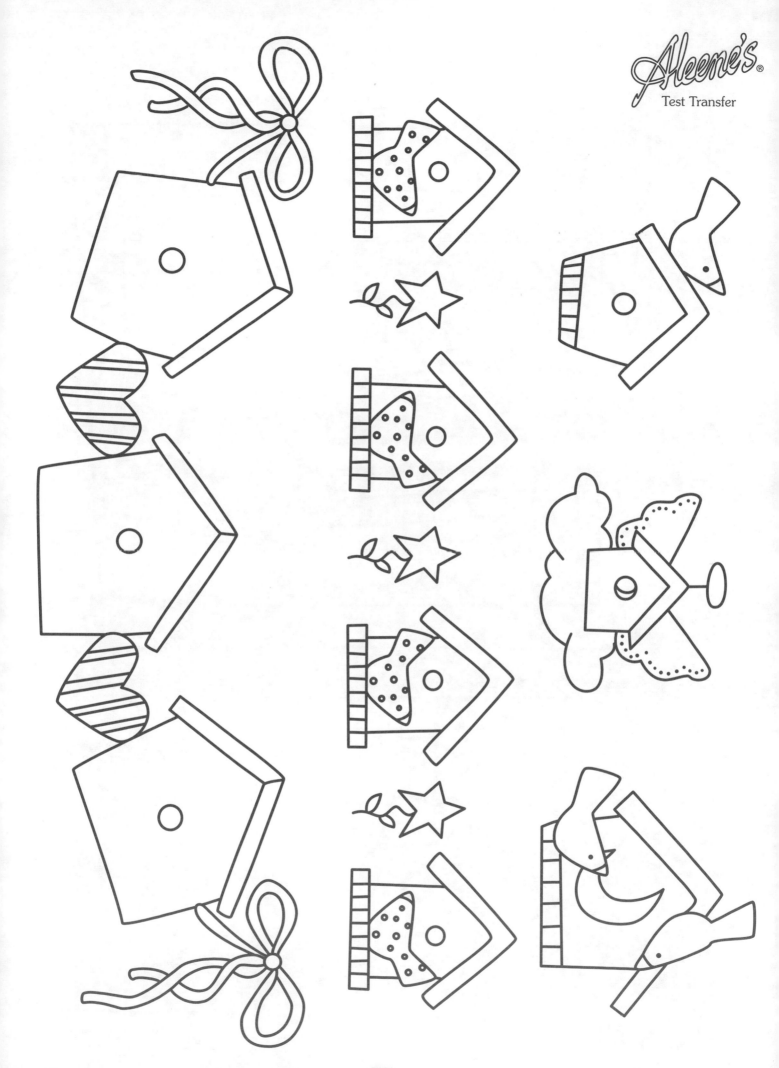

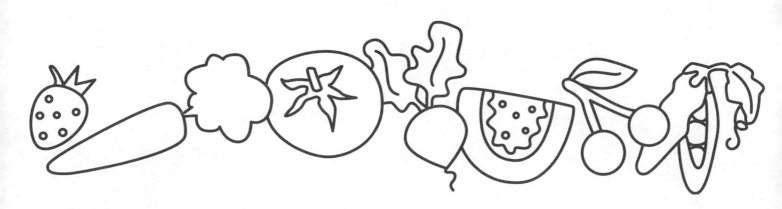

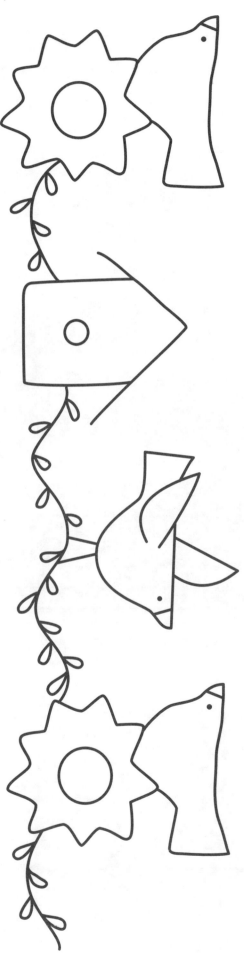

45

Aleene's®
Test Transfer

47

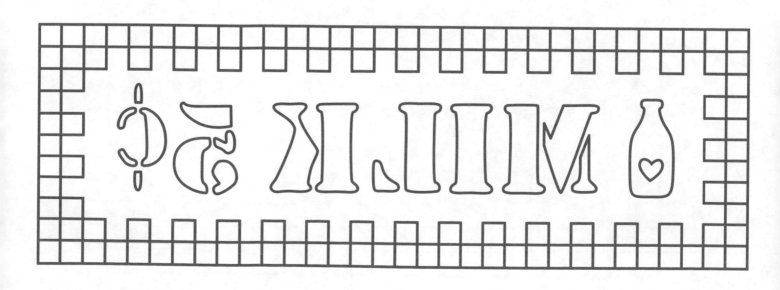

Aleene's®
Test Transfer

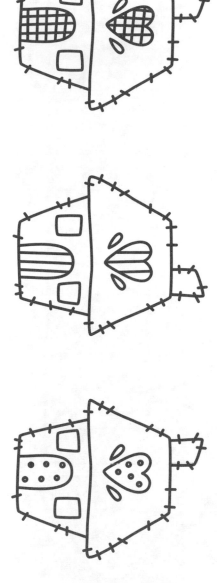

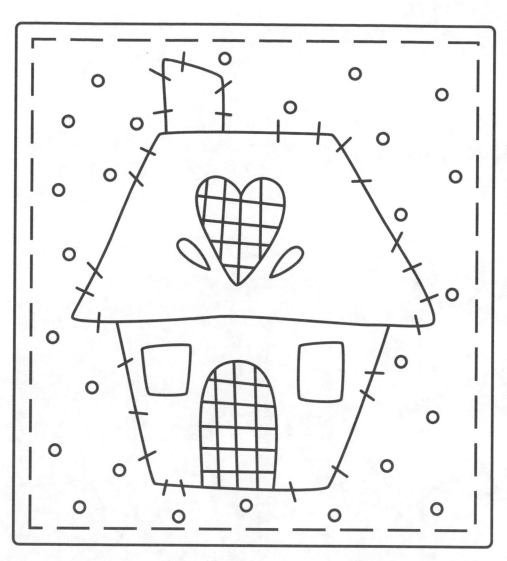

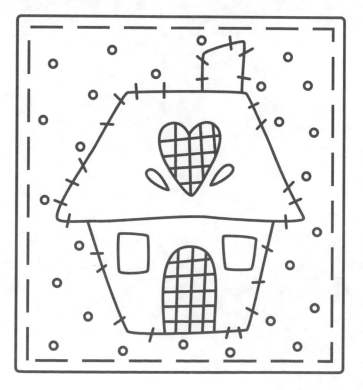

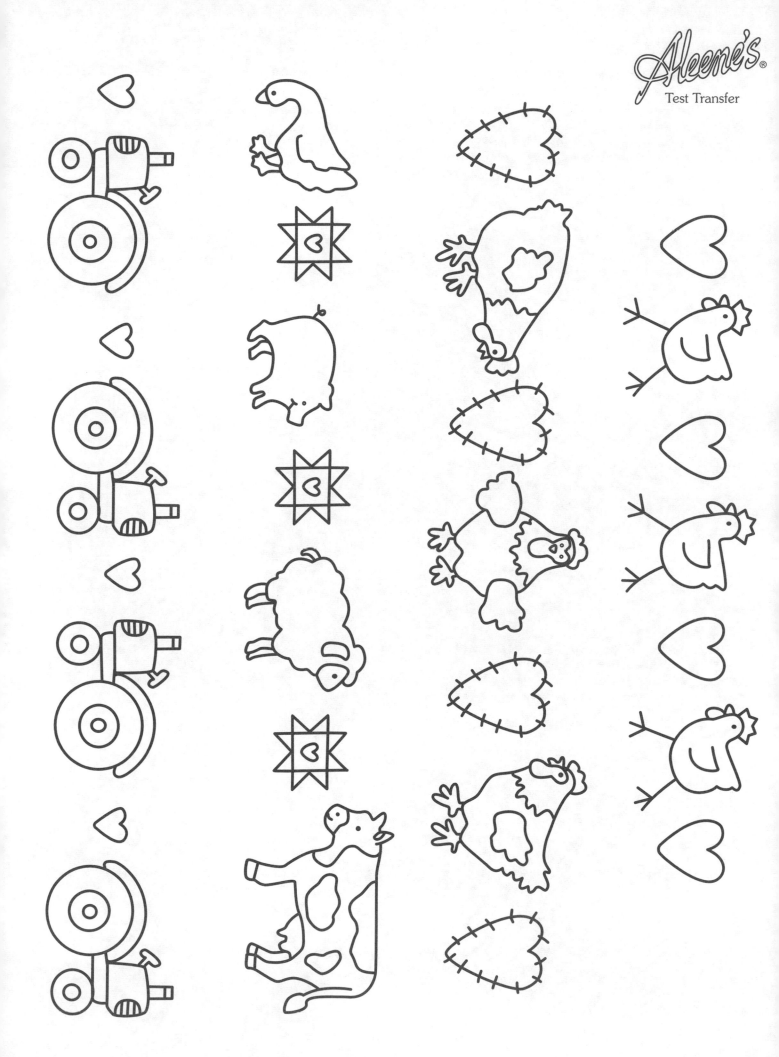

53

APPLE PIE

COUNTRY AT HEART

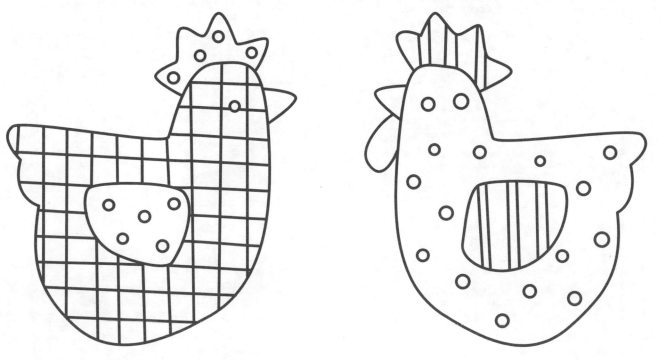

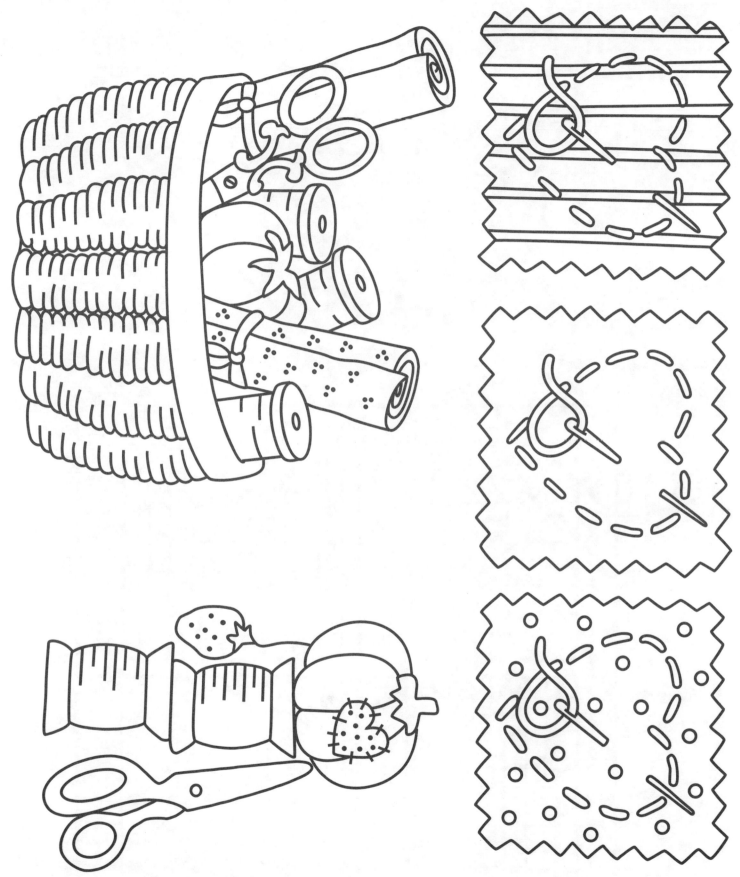

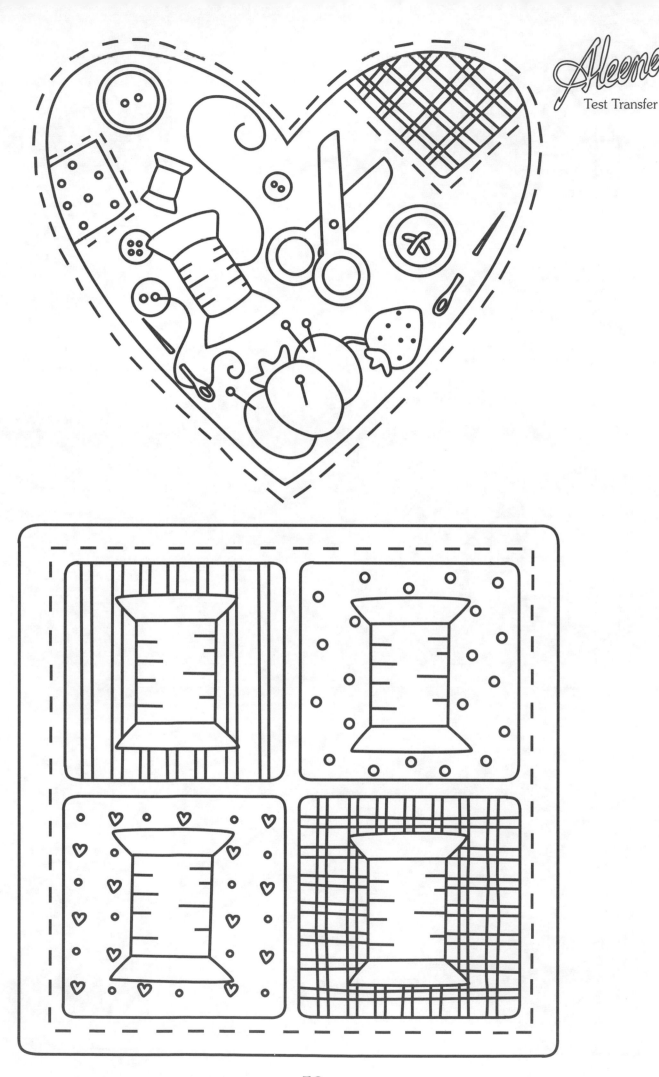

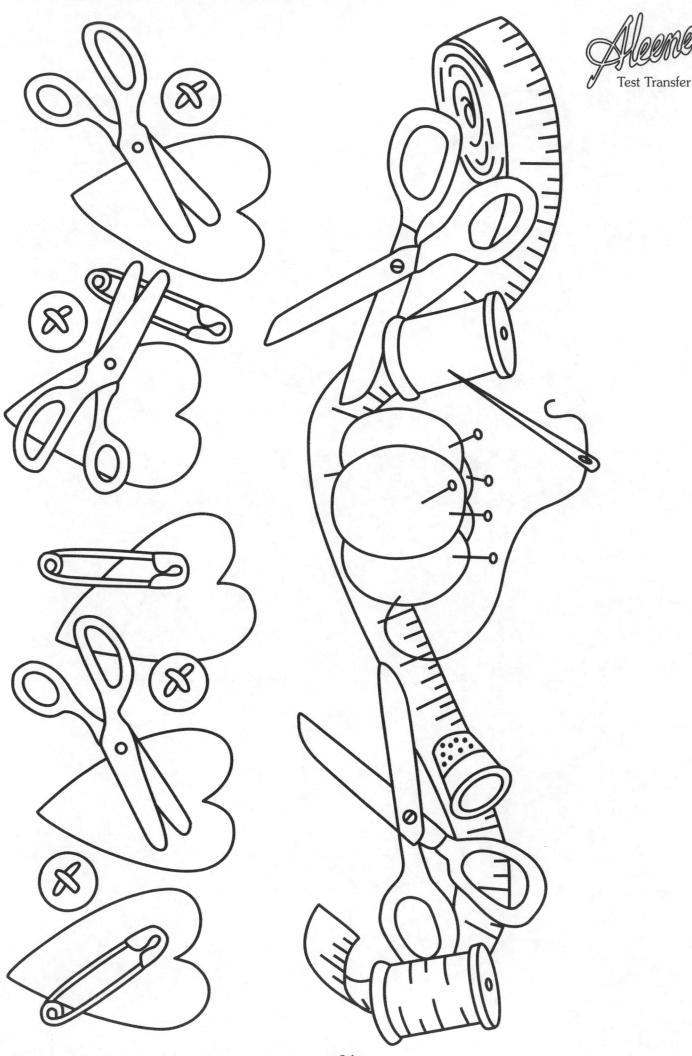

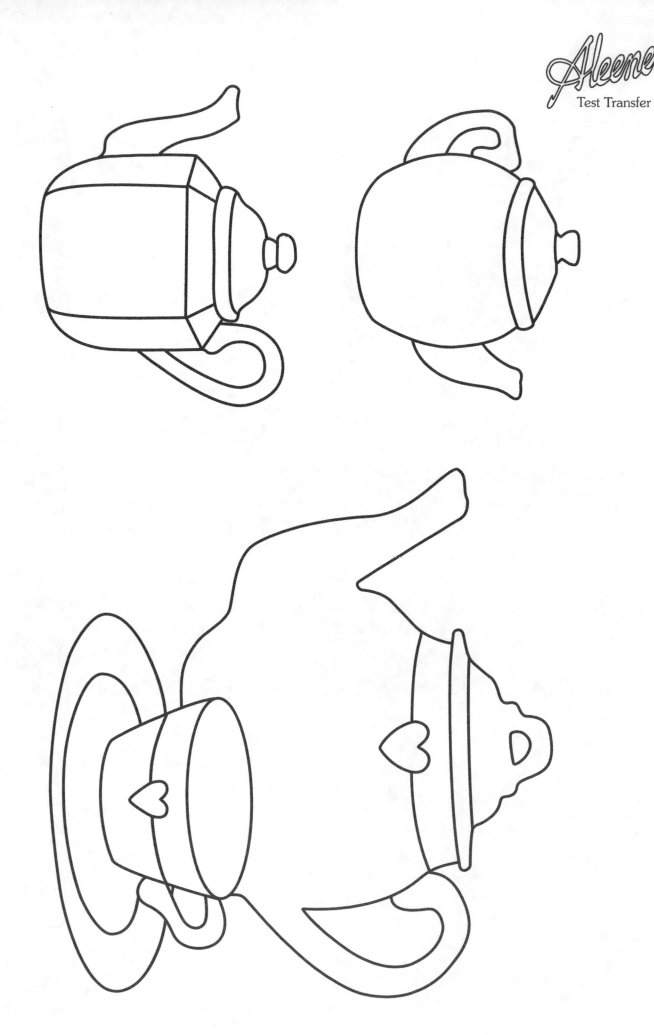

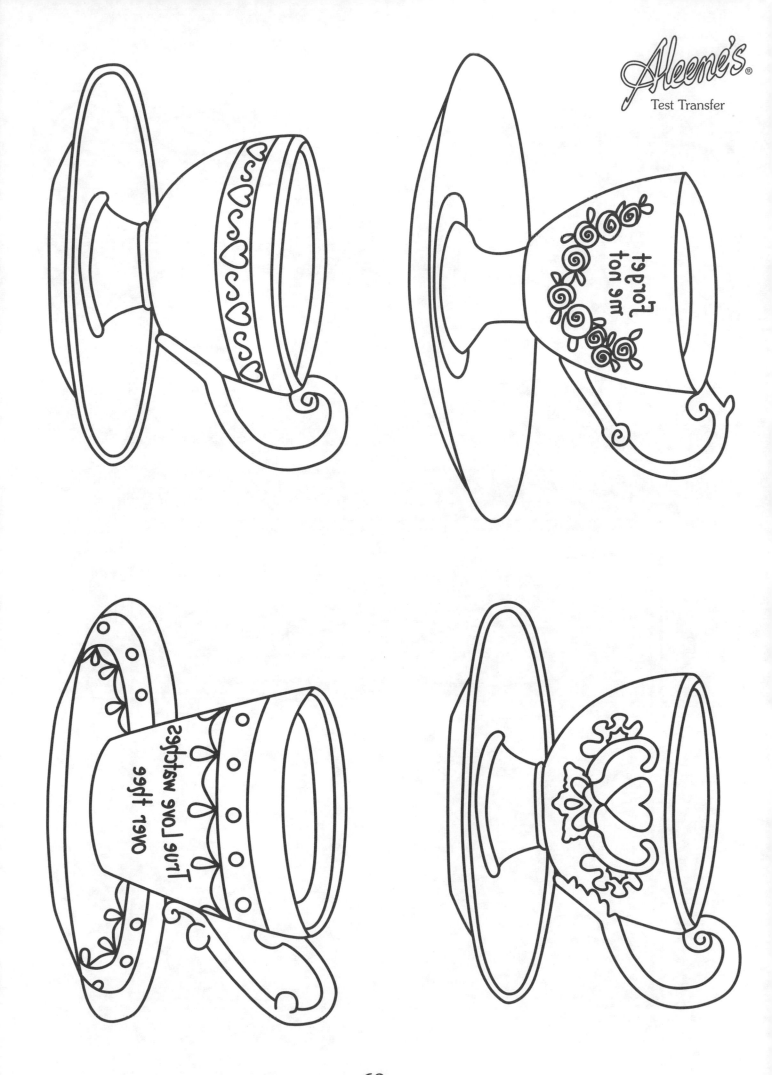

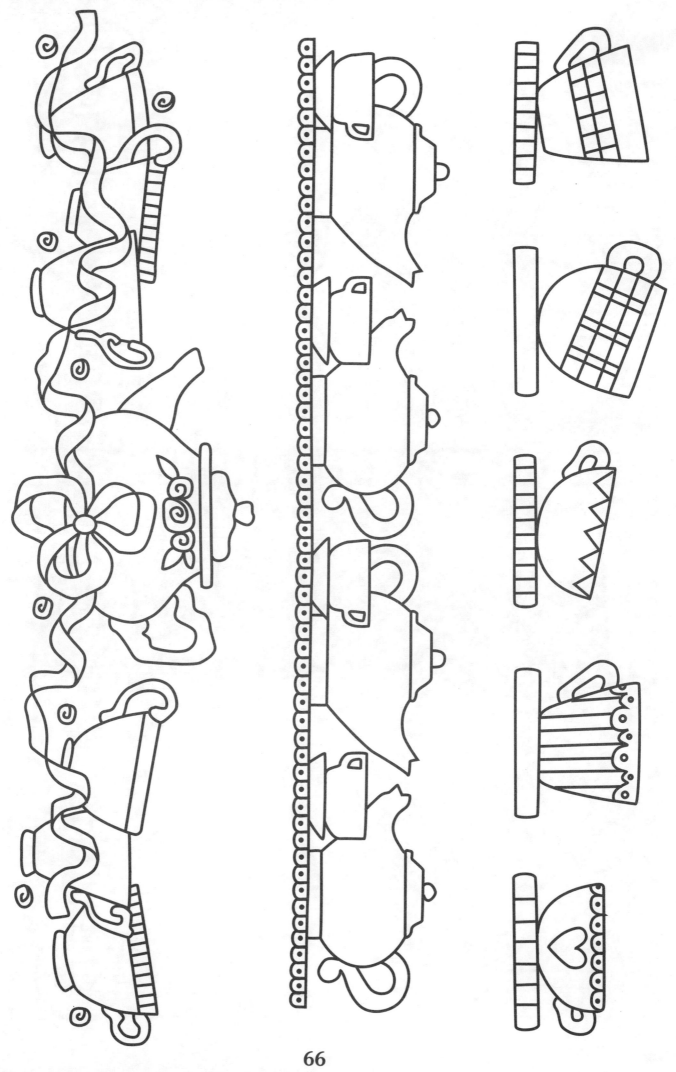

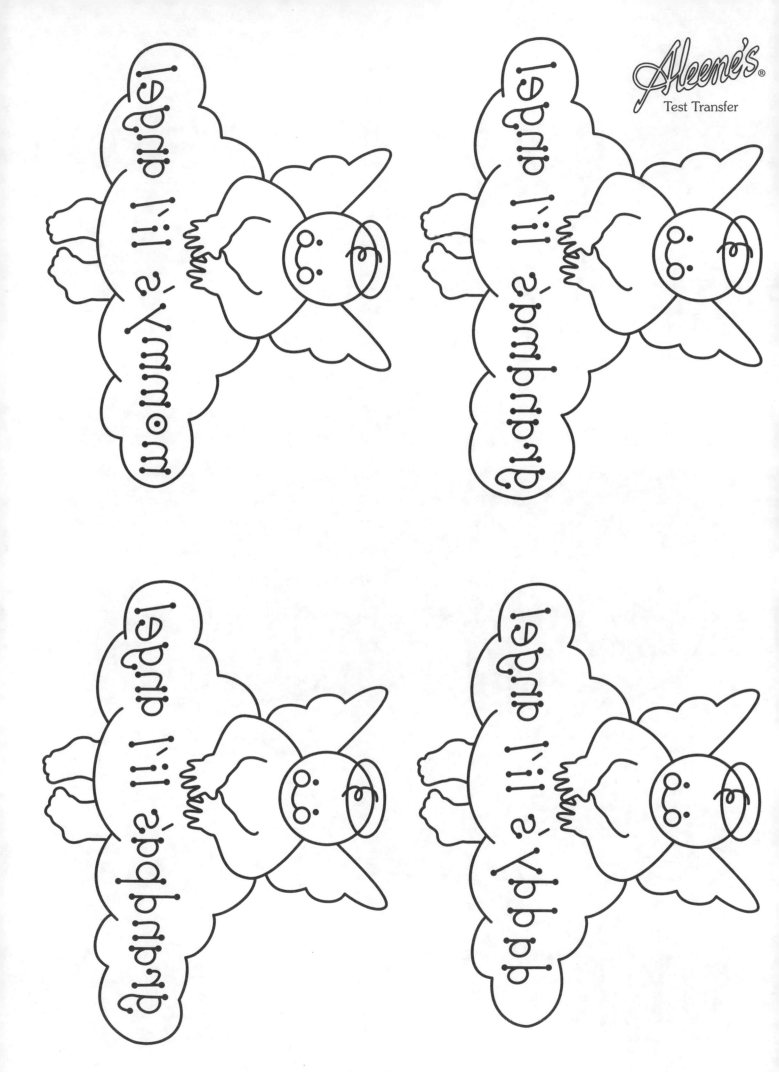

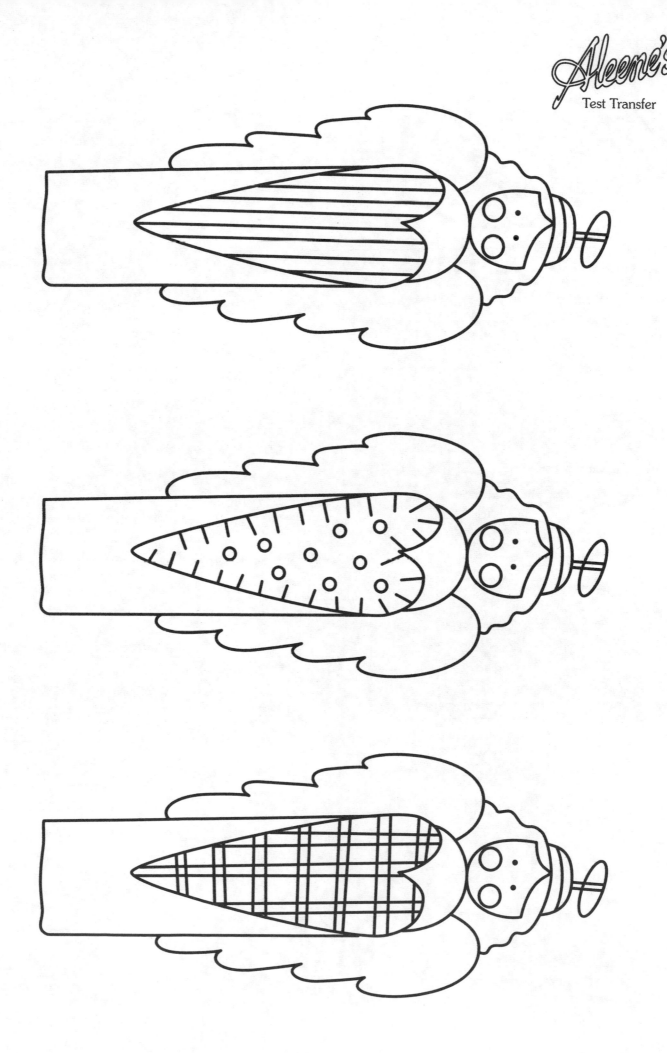

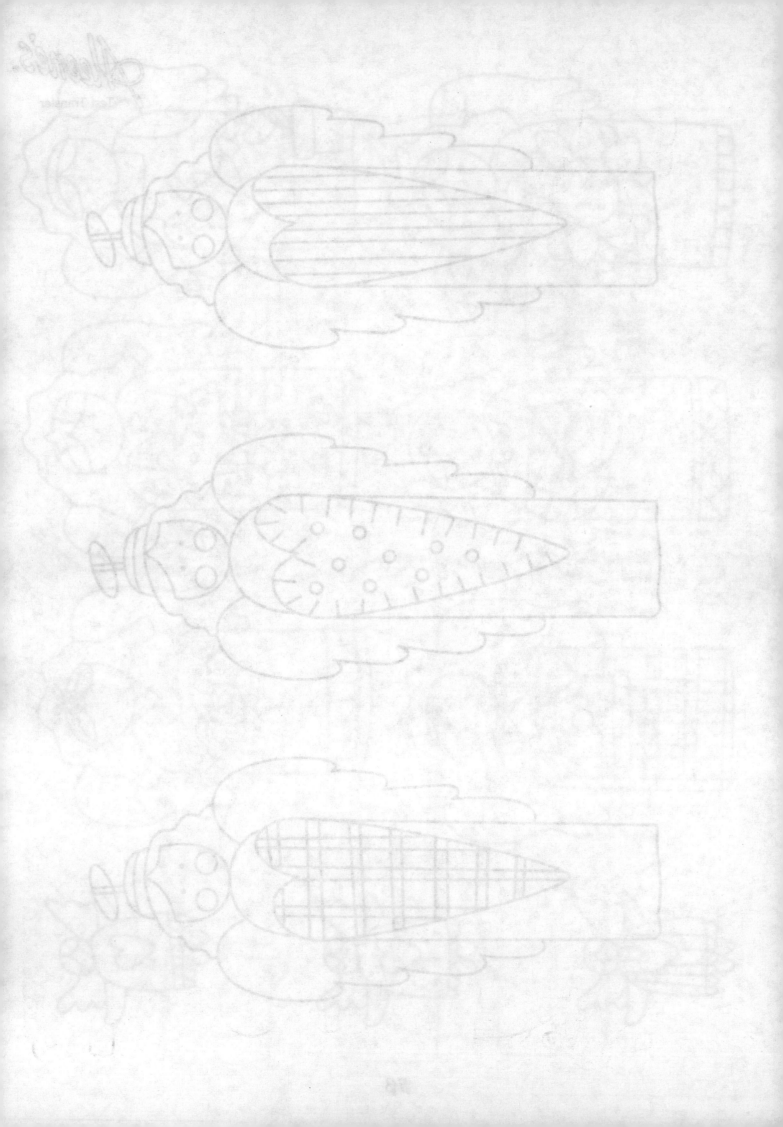

Every little kitten loves nine lives cats

LOVE ME
LOVE MY CAT

MAN'S BEST FRIEND

MAN'S BEST FRIEND

81

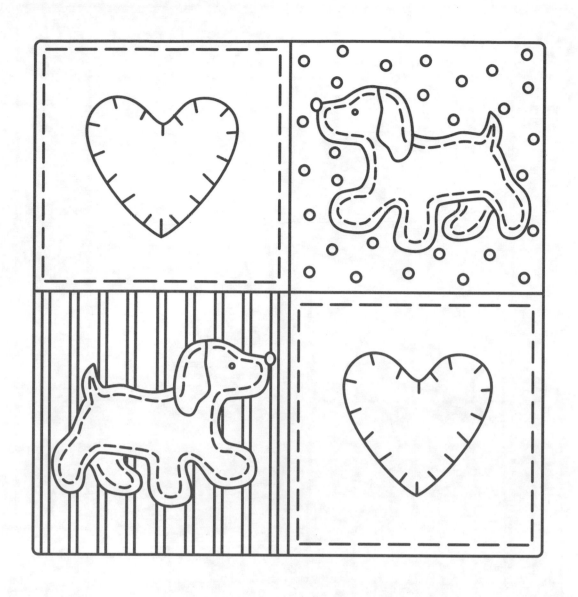

83

ALL CREATURES
GREAT AND SMALL

100

101

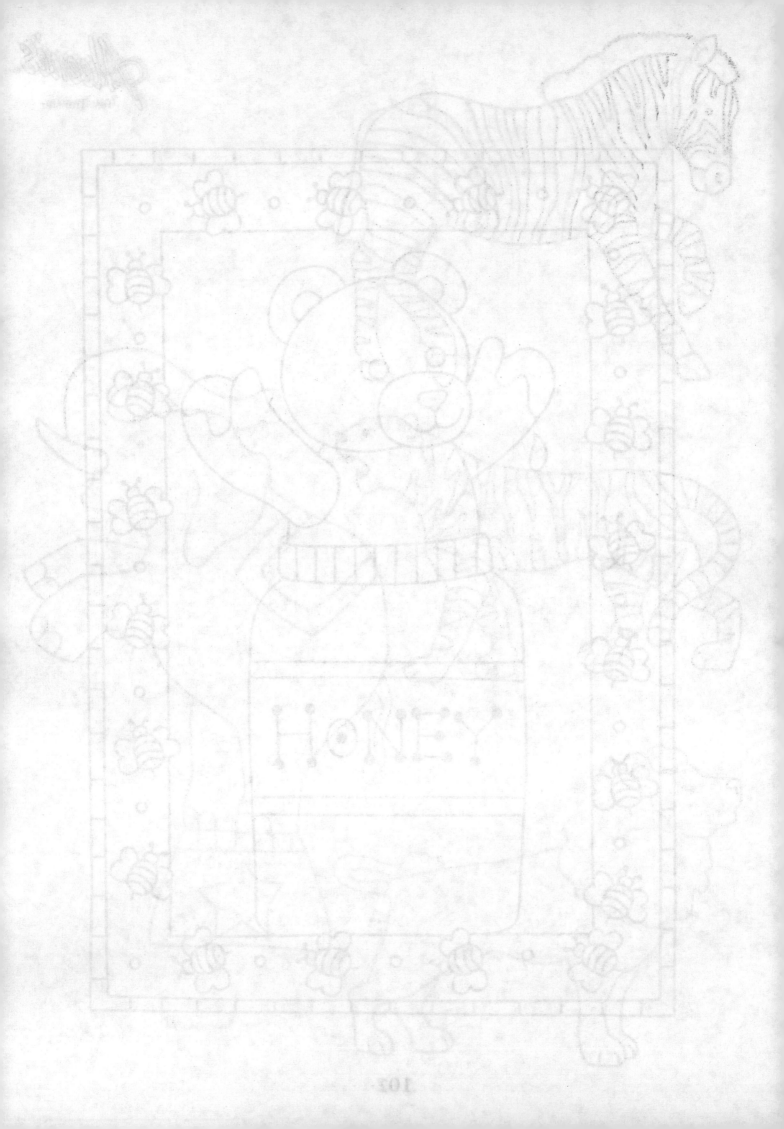

102

Aleene's®
Test Transfer

103

Aleene's®
Test Transfer

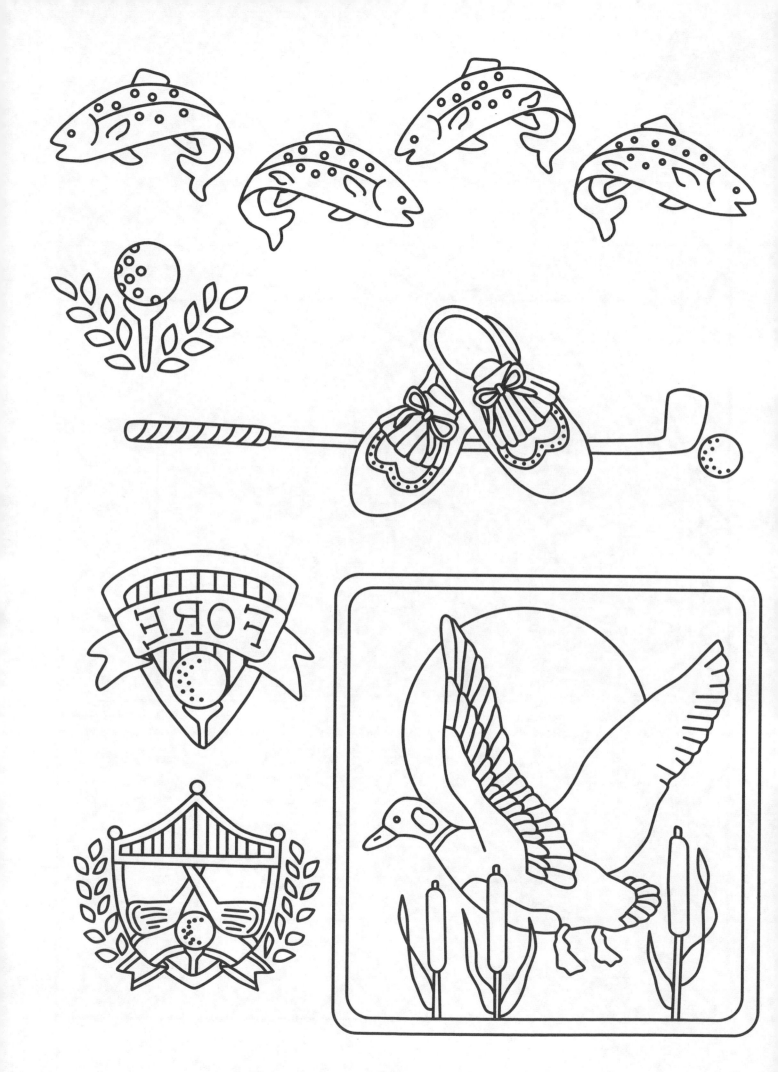

109

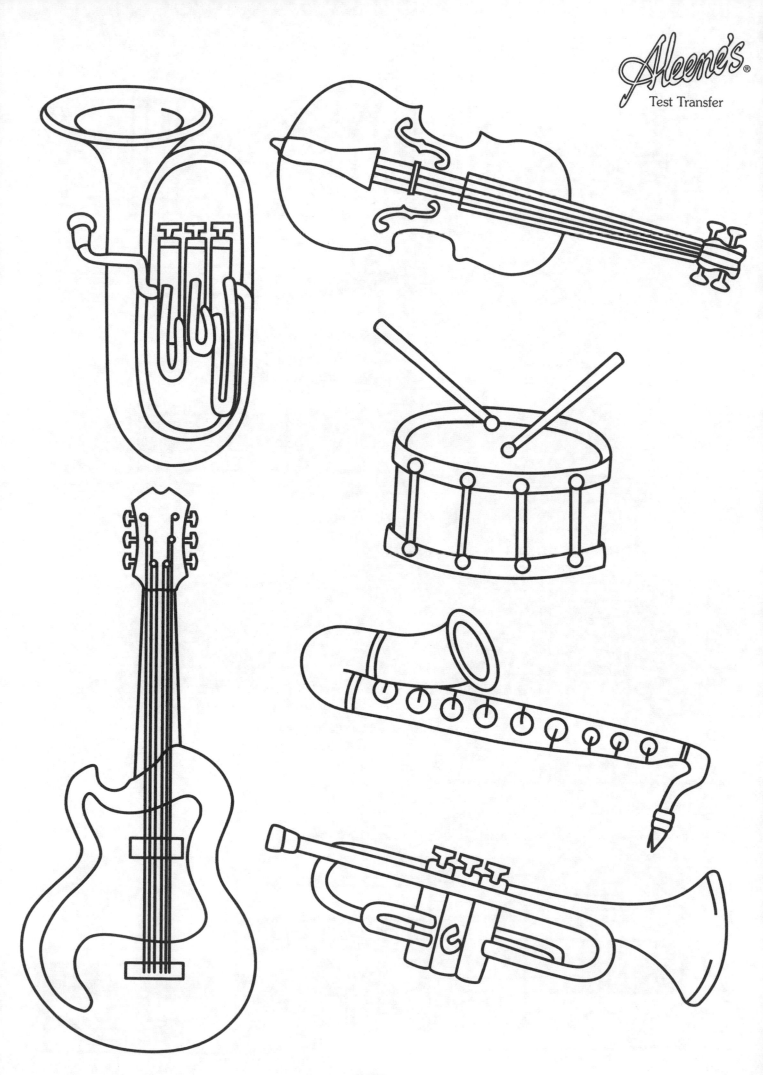

113

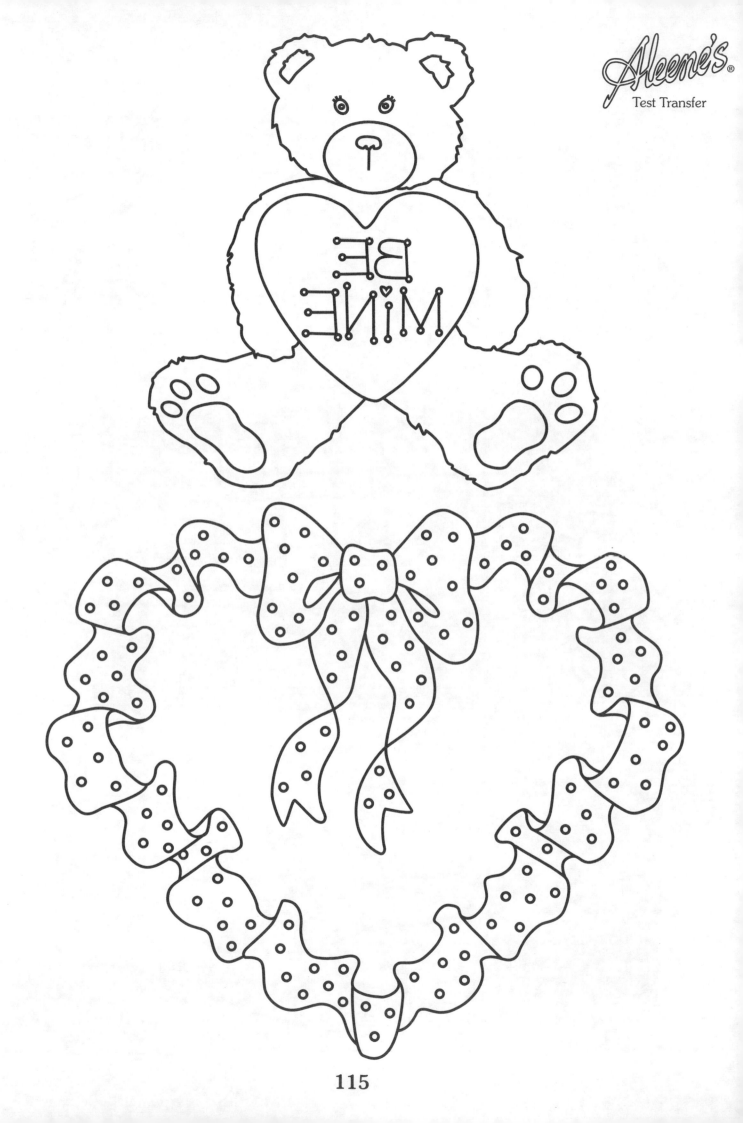

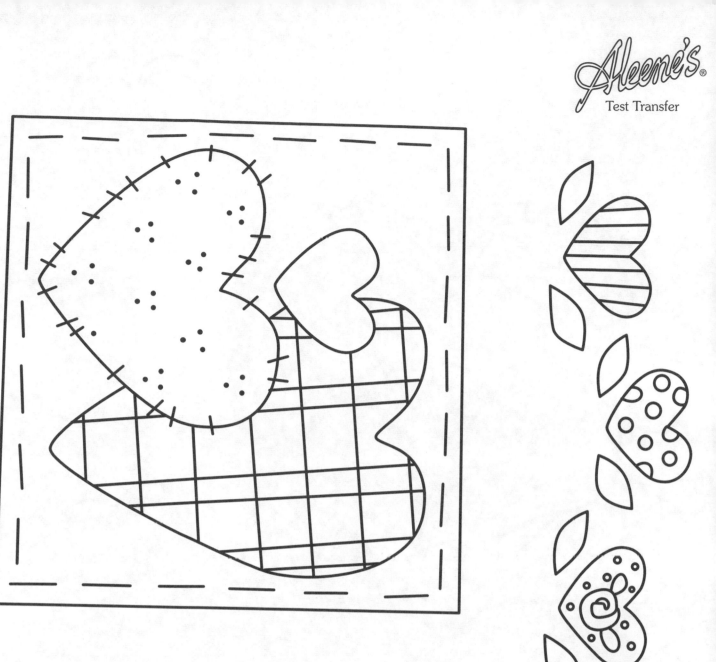

117

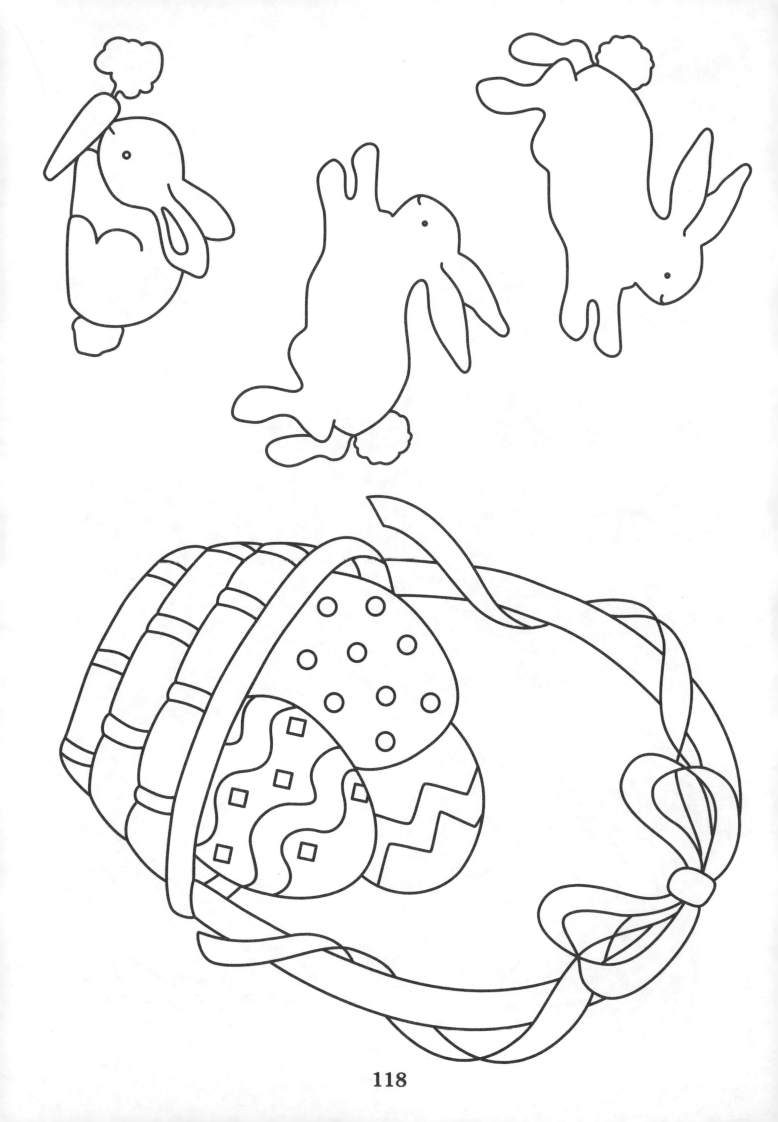

123

Teachers have class!

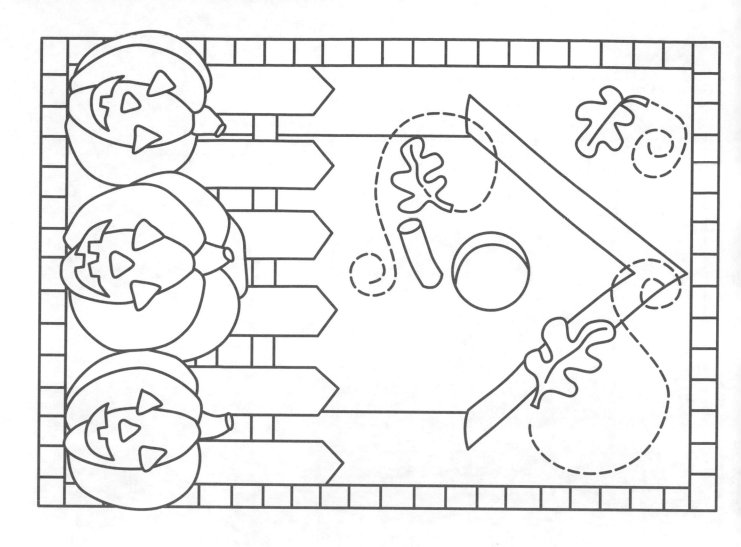

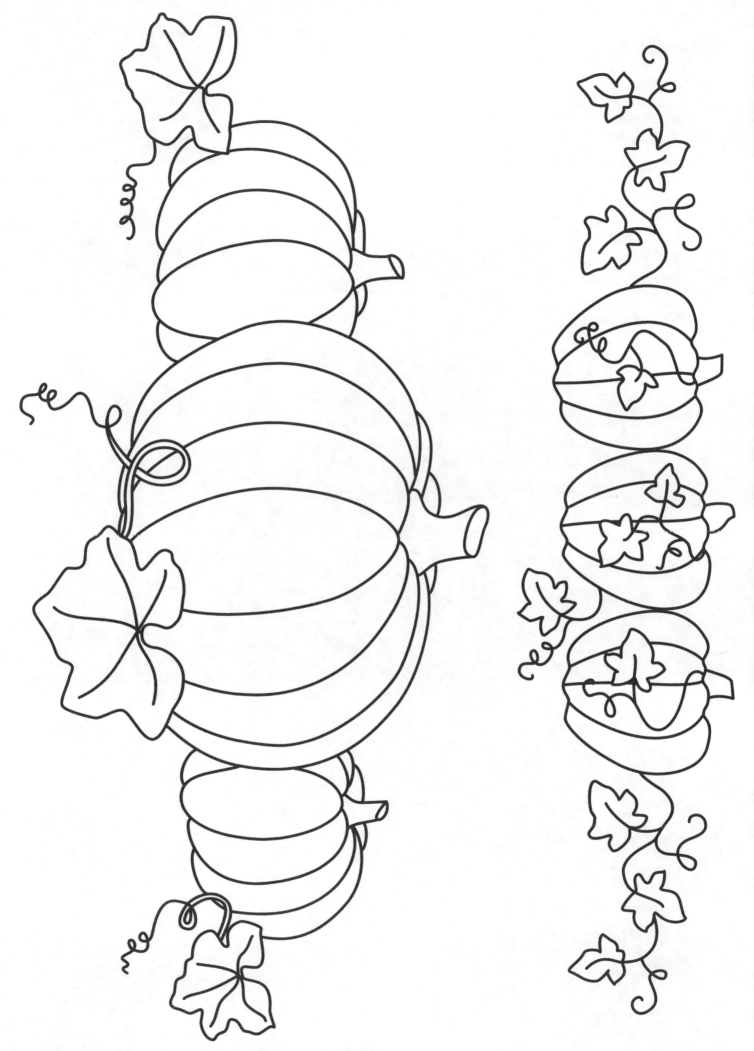

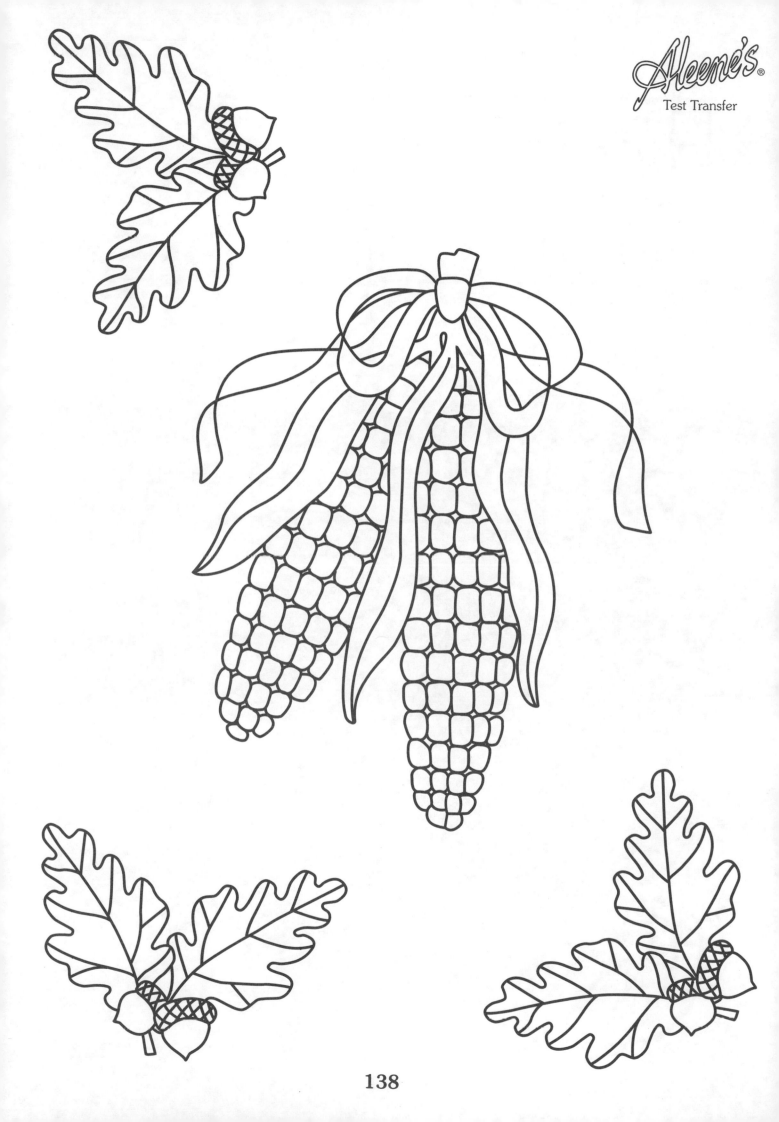

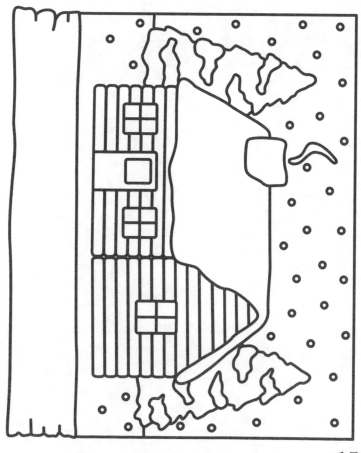

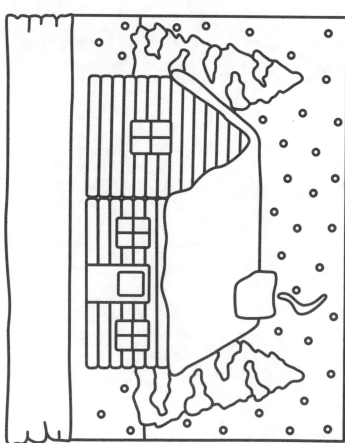

Aleene's®
Test Transfer

155

Aleene's®
Test Transfer

162

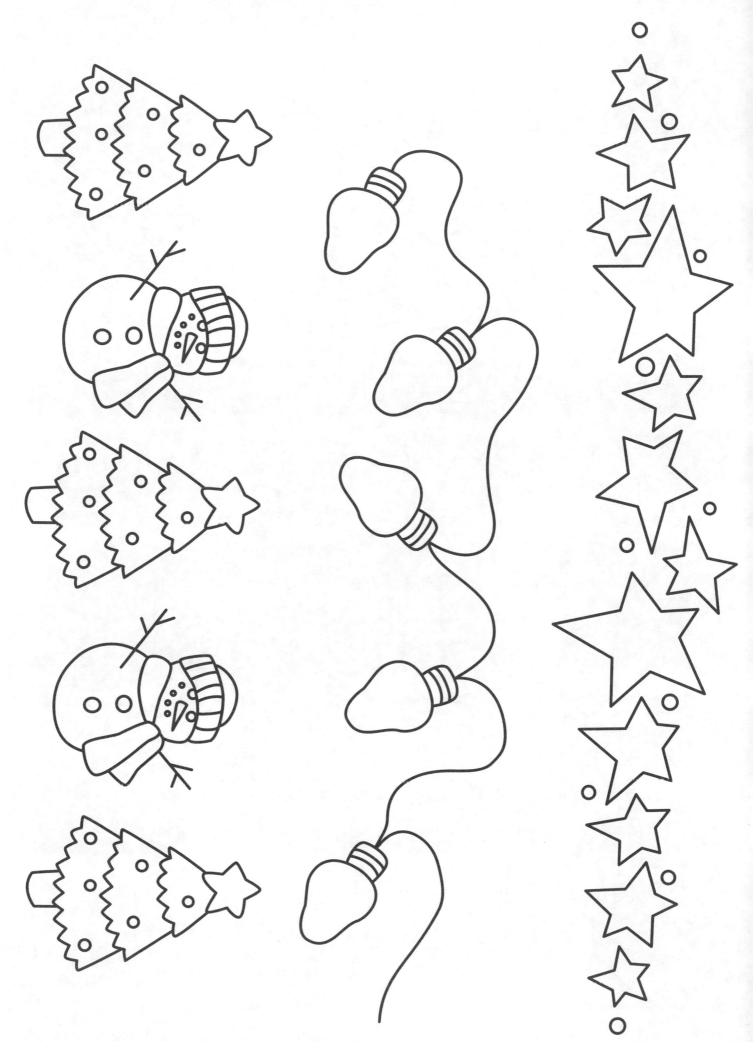

166

Aleene's®
Test Transfer

1234567890

abcdefghijklmn

opqrstuvwxyz

ABCDEF

GHIJKLM

NOPQRST

UVWXYZ

167

A B C D
1 2 3 4 5 6 7 8 9 0

a b c d e f g h i j k l m n
o p q r s t u v w x y z

A B C D E F
G H I J K L M
N O P Q R S T
U V W X Y Z

A B C D

E F G H I

J K L M N

O P Q R S

T U V W

X Y Z

A B C D

1 2 3 4 5 6 7 8 9 0

E F G H I

J K L M N

O P Q R S

T U V W

X Y Z

Aleene's®
Test Transfer

1 2 3 4 5 6 7 8 9 0

a b c d e f g h i j k l
m n o p q r s t u v w x y z

A B C D E
F G H I J K
L M N O P
Q R S T U
V W X Y Z

1 2 3 4 5 6 7 8 9 0

a b c d e f g h i j k l

m n o p q r s t u v w x y z

A B C D E

F G H I J K

L M N O P

Q R S T U

V W X Y Z